We hope you enjoy our cookbook as much as we did making it. Bon appetit!

RECIPES FROM THE GARRISON INN

GENE GARRISON

Anne Marie & Gary

Table of Contents

Table of Contents

Introduction

     Probably one of the most important days of my life (besides the day my son was born or more importantly, the day I asked Anne Marie to marry me) occurred when I first took an interest in learning to cook from my Mother. This started me down a path that I still enjoy to this day.

     My first big challenge came when I was 14 and won the county fair with my chocolate marshmallow meringue pie. And were those little old ladies who were used to winning upset. But I was hooked!!

     It wasn't until my early 20's that I decided to get some professional training and enrolled in the hospitality program at Fanshawe College of London, Ontario. There I took my first cooking classes. I also learned to appreciate the front of the house (the dining room) wine and much more. From there, my career grew: a cook at Pat & Mario's, a waiter at Minaki Lodge, an assistant manager of a restaurant in Manley Beach, Australia, Owner & Operator of Food for Thought Catering, General Manager, Wine Steward at The Chateau Lake Louise, Alberta, Food & Beverage Manager , to where I am now, Owner & Chef of The Garrison Inn.

     This book is a collection of better than 30 years in the kitchen. Many of the recipes I've included have come from experiences from my upbringing, my work experiences, my dining experiences and suggestions from my family and friends.

     As a self-taught chef, I have learned some of my most valuable lessons from watching, tasting, and making mistakes (ask Anne Marie about the pesto on our honeymoon). I taught myself to cook and so can you. Anybody can cook, but the art of cooking is hard to teach. It is not a science, or math, where A + B = C. Experiences, the good and the bad, can teach you how to cook. This book will give you some of the best recipes!

     Please enjoy them, please change them, please…. make them yours.

     I call myself……Chef Gene

The Garrison Inn
406-752-5103

Breakfast

WHOLE WHEAT PANCAKES

Light and fluffy and great with maple syrup. You can use the same batter for waffles as well.

Ingredients:

1 egg

1 tbsp vegetable oil

1 cup whole wheat flour

1 cup milk

1 ½ tsp baking powder

½ tsp salt

Heat griddle (I have a 50 year old cast iron griddle that is seasoned perfectly)

Mix together flour, baking powder and salt

Add oil, egg and milk to dry ingredients and mix well

Make sure griddle is hot. Drops of water will sizzle when the griddle is hot enough

Pour 4" circles of batter on to griddle

Leave room between pancakes as they will expand

When bubbles form and start to pop it is time to flip the pancakes

Remove from griddle when both sides are brown

Serve hot with butter and syrup

Makes 8 – 10 pancakes

EGGS BENEDICT

This is one of Anne Marie's favorite breakfast meals. They make a great brunch item worth the extra effort.

Ingredients:	Hollandaise sauce:
8 eggs	3 eggs
4 English muffins	½ lb. butter
8 slices Canadian bacon	Juice of a lemon
	1 tsp Dijon mustard
	¼ tsp ground white pepper
	1 dash of Tabasco
	Pinch of salt
	1 tsp white vinegar

To make the Hollandaise sauce:

Fill a medium sauce pan ¾ full of water and bring to a boil

Separate the 3 eggs into whites and yokes then place the yokes into a medium metal bowl

that is capable of fitting over the sauce pan

If you can use them within the same day, save the egg whites

Add mustard, pepper, Tabasco, lemon juice and salt to egg yokes and stir to mix

Over boiling water, slowly cook egg mixture until it starts to thicken

DO NOT OVERCOOK EGGS. Meanwhile, melt the butter

Once eggs have thickened, remove from heat and slowly whisk in melted butter

Set Hollandaise sauce aside

Pre-heat broiler

Cut English muffins in half on the seam then toast them

Lightly butter muffins and keep warm

Warm Canadian bacon in microwave

Add vinegar to boiling water

Break remaining eggs one at a time into a small dish then pour egg into the water to poach

Eggs are done when firm but the yoke should still be runny

To build Eggs Benedict, take ½ English muffin, then a slice of bacon and top with poached egg

To finish, top with Hollandaise sauce and arrange on a baking sheet

If Hollandaise sauce is too thick it can be thinned with a little water

Once all the Eggs Benedict have been built, brown tops under broiler

Serve 2 Eggs Benedict per plate

Makes 4 servings

FLUFFY OMELET

This is NOT your typical omelet. This omelet swells to almost twice its size when finished cooking and has the texture of a soufflé. The omelet can be filled with a variety of different ingredients.

Ingredients:

3 eggs

½ of a ¼" slice of country ham

2 tbsp diced green onion

Cooking spray

1 tbsp butter

2 tbsp diced green pepper

½ cup shredded cheddar and mozzarella cheese

In a small frying pan melt butter

Dice ham, green peppers and onion

Sauté in butter until peppers have softened and ham is warmed through

Remove from heat and set aside

Separate egg whites and yokes

Beat egg whites until they form peaks

Beat yokes until smooth

Fold yokes into egg whites

Fold ham, green peppers, onion and cheese into egg mixture

Spray omelet pan with cooking spray and add egg mixture

Cook over lowest heat setting possible until eggs set 15 – 20 minutes

Heat broiler while eggs are cooking

Once eggs have set, brown top of omelet under broiler

Slide omelet out of pan onto serving plate and fold in half

Serve hot with toast

Makes 1 serving

STUFFED FRENCH TOAST

The Stuffed French Toast is one of the most popular breakfast dishes here at The Garrison Inn.

Ingredients:

1 loaf French bread frozen

2 beaten eggs

1 tbsp brandy

½ cup half & half

Huckleberry, raspberry or apricot jam (we make our own)! Heat griddle

Microwave bread 30 seconds until soft, but still slightly frozen

Cut bread into ½" slices, keeping slices in order

Microwave bread an additional 30 seconds or until thawed

Take 2 side-by-side slices and spread jam on one slice then cover with the other slice

Continue forming French toast until bread is gone

In a cake pan or shallow dish add eggs, brandy and half & half and mix together

Dip French toast in egg mixture making sure to cover both sides

Cook on hot griddle until browned on one side

Turn and cook the other side

Serve 2 pieces of toast per order

Makes 3 – 4 servings

Comments from The Garrison Inn

July / 31 /2003
Fantastic view - accommodations were great. The lodge is beautiful as well as peaceful. The company was a pleasure - getting to know about the area was a special unexpected benefit. Our daughter and her husband, JoLonna and Rian couldn't say enough good things about it - Your lodge has been the discussion at all the wedding functions - the " oh you're the people staying at the Inn! " has been the comments we've heard all week. Letting us keep" Buster" was especially nice - He really enjoyed driving in & getting to sniff about. Thanks for everything.

John and Jodee Pendleton, OR

July / 31 /2003
Thanks for a peaceful spot to rejuvenate ourselves after a whirl wind week of wedding preparations. The accommodations were wonderful. Mike & Cathy Portland, OR

Sept. / 17 - 19 / 2004
Thank you for a beautiful weekend! We truly enjoyed every aspect of our stay...your wonderful hospitality, magnificent home & view, fantastic breakfasts, and our play-time with Gray. He is a loveable young boy! Thanks for your hospitality and for opening your home to us.

Brad and Charlotte, Calgary, Alberta, Canada

Oct. / 24 / 2004
Thank you for your generous hospitality. We enjoyed The Garrison Inn, your home and family so much. You made it very comfortable for us. The bed is terrific, the view and the food worth every penny.

Allison & Bob, Mendham, NJ

Jan. / 01 / 2005
Thanks for sharing your wonderful house. It's like coming home when we stay with you. As the first patrons, we take pride in coming back to visit. We will remember bringing in the New Year 2005. Thanks again for everything!!   Jolonna & Rian, Portland, OR

June / 30 / 2005
Peaceful, warm, relaxing and capped with majestic views,including your beautiful home with its lofty ceilings. Thank you so much for your hospitality & kindness. You truly made me feel like I was staying in a home away from home. Keep up the great work!   Dan, Milwaukee, WI

August / 11 / 2005
What a fabulous spot! We appreciated your warm hospitality. Your food & wine were just great. Hopefully we'll return for a longer stay   Diane & Duncan, Ottawa Ont. Canada

Starters

ROASTED RED PEPPER SOUP

By far, this is Anne Marie's favorite soup. She has me make extra and freeze it every time. I told her to make her own, but she tried it once and said mine was better. I just think she wants me to make it.

Ingredients:

1 medium onion chopped	1 tbsp dried fennel seed
¾ cup olive oil	¼ tsp dried thyme
¼ tsp crushed bay leaf	1 tsp minced garlic
1 tbsp chopped fresh basil or ½ tsp dried	2 tbsp chopped jalapeno peppers
¼ cup flour	5 cups chicken stock
½ cup chopped fresh tomato	1 tsp tomato paste
6 large red peppers	½ cup half & half
1 cup whipping cream	1 tsp sugar
Salt	Fresh ground pepper
Sambuca	

Soup:

In a large heavy-bottomed sauce pan, heat ½ cup olive oil over medium heat

Add chopped onion, fennel, thyme, bay leaf, garlic, basil and jalapeno peppers

Reduce heat to low and cook 10 – 15 minutes or until onions are tender

Add flour and cook 10 minutes stirring constantly

In a separate pot bring chicken stock to a boil. Slowly pour stock over vegetables stirring well

Add tomatoes and tomato paste and let simmer. Cut peppers into 2" squares. In a large frying pan heat 1 tbsp olive oil per batch. Char peppers in oil in batches then add to the soup

Simmer soup 20 minutes. Remove soup from heat and puree in small batches in a blender or food processor. Strain soup to remove pulp. Return soup to heat and add half & half, sugar, salt and pepper to taste. Bring soup back to temperature

Topping:

Whip cream to form peaks, add pinch of sugar and 3 tbsp Sambuca

To serve:

Add splash of Sambuca to bottom of soup bowl. Fill bowl with soup

Add a dollop of whipped cream. Garnish with fresh basil leaves

Makes 8 servings

FRENCH ONION SOUP

On a cold winter's day, this soup warms the soul, and is best if cooked slowly all day.

Ingredients:

8 cups water
8 tsp McCormick's beef base
¼ cup cooking sherry
3 large yellow onions
¼ tsp ground white pepper
6 slices French bread
2 cups shredded Jarlsberg or Swiss cheese

Notes:
I prefer McCormick's, but you can use your favorite base / bouillon to make 8 cups of beef stock. For the cheese, my favorite is Jarlsberg, but you can also use Emmentaler or Gruyere.

In a sauce pan, bring 8 cups of water to a boil. Add beef base and dissolve
Transfer stock to a slow cooker on medium heat. Cut onions into slices ¼" thick and add to the stock
Add pepper and sherry and simmer all day
Pre-heat the broiler. On a baking sheet arrange soup bowls
Add 1 tsp cooking sherry to each bowl
Fill bowls with onion soup. Make sure to get lots of onions in each bowl
Top with a slice of French bread with the crust removed
Sprinkle 1/3 cup cheese over soup
Melt cheese under broiler
Enjoy!
Makes 6 servings

POTATO LEEK SOUP

Potato leek soup is one of our favorites and can be made in an hour or less.

Ingredients:

1 large or 2 small leeks

20 black peppercorns

2 tbsp butter

½ cup dry white wine

4 cups chicken stock

¾ tsp ground white pepper

2 bay leaves

1 tsp dried thyme

2 strips bacon chopped

4 large potatoes diced

1 ½ tsp salt

½ cup half and half

Trim off the green portion of the leek saving the 2 largest and longest leaves

Make a bouquet garni by folding the 2 leaves around the bay leaves, peppercorns and thyme

Tie into a package-shaped bundle with kitchen twine and set aside

Alternately tie the leek leaves, bay leaves, peppercorns and thyme together in a piece of cheesecloth

Halve the white part of the leeks and rinse well

Slice the leeks thinly crosswise and set aside

In a large soup pot, melt the butter over medium heat

Add bacon and cook 5 minutes or until most of the fat is rendered

Add the chopped leeks and cook 5 minutes

Add wine and bring to a boil

Add the bouquet garni, chicken stock, potatoes, salt and pepper and bring back to a boil

Reduce heat to simmer and cook 30 minutes

Remove the bouquet garni. Puree the soup in a blender

Stir in the half and half

Serves 4

CAESAR SALAD

It's the dressing that makes a great Caesar salad and I have been making this one for more than 20 years. I make it in a large batch and then store it in the fridge. This salad is great as is, or for a change, just add chicken or beef.

Ingredients:

1 head romaine lettuce	½ cup croutons
1/3 cup grated parmesan cheese	½ of a lemon
3 egg yokes	½ tsp salt
½ tsp pepper	5 anchovy filets
4 tsp chopped garlic	2 tsp Dijon mustard
1 tsp Worcestershire sauce	¼ tsp Tabasco sauce
1/8 cup red wine vinegar	1 ½ cups vegetable oil

To make the dressing:
On a cutting board spread the salt and top with the anchovies
Using the blade of a knife, mash the anchovies into a paste
Place the anchovies into a large mixing bowl
Add the egg yokes, pepper, garlic, mustard, Worcestershire, Tabasco and vinegar
Slowly whisk in the oil until you get a creamy dressing. Store in the fridge

To build the salad:
Rinse lettuce under cold water and shake off excess water. Tear lettuce into bite size pieces. Place lettuce in a large mixing bowl. Add 1/3 – 1/2 cup Caesar dressing
Add juice of ½ lemon, parmesan cheese and croutons. Toss until well mixed

Serves 4

ORIENTAL CHICKEN AND SPINACH SALAD

We do this salad as a meal. It makes for a light meal and is great, especially in the summer.

Ingredients:

¼ cup vegetable oil

3 tbsp rice vinegar

1 ½ tbsp sugar

1 tbsp soy sauce

1 tsp dark sesame oil

¾ tsp grated gingerroot

6 oz baby spinach leaves

2 cups cooked cubed chicken breast

1 can (11 oz) mandarin oranges, drained

½ cup sliced water chestnuts

¼ cup thinly sliced green onions

¼ cup slivered almonds

½ cup chow mein noodles (optional)

Whisk together oil, vinegar, sugar, soy sauce, sesame oil and ginger

Refrigerate covered for at least 1 hour

In a large mixing bowl toss the spinach, chicken, oranges, water chestnuts, onion, almonds and chow mein noodles with the dressing

Serves 4

GREEK SALAD

Greek salad is a rough-country salad of juicy tomatoes, crisp cucumbers, onions, green peppers, crumbly feta cheese and plump olives. Serve this delightful combination as a side dish or as a light meal with some crusty bread.

Ingredients:

3 tbsp olive oil

1½ tbsp red wine vinegar

1 tsp minced garlic

½ tsp dried oregano

¼ tsp salt

¼ tsp fresh ground pepper

1 large chopped tomato

1 small chopped onion

½ cucumber chopped

½ green pepper chopped

4 oz feta cheese cut into small cubes

16 kalamata olives cut in half (or black olives will do nicely)

Combine oil, vinegar, garlic, oregano, salt and pepper in a sealable container and shake to mix

Place the tomato, onion, cucumber, green pepper, feta and olives in a mixing bowl

Pour the dressing over the salad and toss

Serve right away

Serves 4

TACO SALAD

Fast and fun faux Mexican food. Everybody in the family loves this salad.

Ingredients:

1 bag regular corn chips
1 lb ground beef
¼ cup taco seasoning
¾ cup water
1 head Romaine lettuce
1 medium tomato
1 cup shredded cheddar and mozzarella cheese mixture
½ cup chopped black olives
1 cup guacamole
1 cup salsa
1 cup sour cream

Brown the beef in a large sauté pan. Drain any fat
Return to heat
Add taco seasoning and water
Simmer until liquid evaporates
Shred the lettuce. On 4 plates, spread the shredded lettuce
Top with corn chips. Divide the meat between the 4 plates
Chop the tomato and spread on top of the meat
Add cheese and top with guacamole, salsa, sour cream and olives

Makes 4 dinner salads

CAPRESE

Caprese is traditionally a salad, normally without vinegar, but I serve it as an appetizer with Balsamic vinegar.

Ingredients:

½ loaf French baguette

1 tbsp olive oil

8 oz ball fresh mozzarella cheese

2 ripe Roma tomatoes

20 fresh basil leaves

3 tbsp olive oil

1 tbsp Balsamic vinegar

Heat griddle

Slice the baguette into ¼" slices

Drizzle baguette slices on both sides with 1 tbsp olive oil

Grill on both sides until lightly browned

Slice tomatoes and cheese into ¼" slices

On a plate arrange the tomatoes and cheese slices, alternating slices

Add the basil leaves

Drizzle the remaining olive oil and the vinegar over the tomatoes and cheese

Add the grilled bread to the plate

Makes 4 – 6 appetizers

CROUSTADE OF MUSHROOMS

Rich and creamy is the best way to describe this appetizer. The Croustade is a small loaf of bread hollowed out then deep-fried golden brown and filled with a creamy mushroom sauce and topped with Hollandaise.

Ingredients:

1 loaf French bread
6 oz baby portabella mushrooms (**Creminis**)
1 tbsp butter
1 tbsp brandy
½ cup whipping cream
½ tsp dried tarragon

Hollandaise:

3 eggs
½ lb. butter
Juice of a lemon
1 tsp Dijon mustard
¼ tsp ground white pepper
1 dash of Tabasco
Pinch of salt
1 tsp white vinegar

To make the Hollandaise sauce:
Fill a medium sauce pan ¾ full of water and bring to a boil
Separate the 3 eggs into whites and yokes then place yokes into a medium metal bowl that is capable of fitting over the sauce pan. If you can use them within the same day, save the egg whites.
Add mustard, pepper, Tabasco, lemon juice and salt to egg yokes and stir to mix. Over boiling water, slowly cook egg mixture until it starts to thicken. **DO NOT OVERCOOK EGGS!** Meanwhile melt the butter. Once eggs have thickened, remove from heat and slowly whisk in melted butter
Set the hollandaise sauce aside

To make mushroom cream sauce:
Slice mushrooms. Melt butter in a sauce pan
Add mushrooms and sauté until tender. Deglaze with brandy
Add cream and tarragon. Stir over medium heat until sauce is nice and creamy

To make croustade:

Pre-heat broiler and deep-fryer to 350 degrees. Cut bread into 3" cubes then hollow out center
Deep-fry bread until golden brown. Fill fried bread with mushroom sauce then top with
Hollandaise sauce. Brown top in broiler

Makes 4 – 6 appetizers

JAMAICAN PATTIES

These can be made either as a snack / appetizer or as a meal, and they freeze well. A little taste of the Caribbean.

Ingredients:

For the filling:

2 tbsp butter	1 large chopped onion
6 cloves minced garlic	1 tbsp finely chopped fresh ginger
¼ tsp dried turmeric	¾ tsp ground cumin
1 tsp cinnamon	½ tsp cardamom
1 finely chopped habanero pepper	1 tsp dried thyme
3 finely chopped green onions	1 tbsp freshly chopped parsley
2 medium chopped ripe tomatoes	1 ½ tsp salt
Ground pepper	¾ cup beef stock
3 tbsp dark rum	2 beaten egg yokes, 1 tbsp dark rum for egg wash

For the pastry:

2 ½ cups flour
½ tsp salt
2 tsp dried turmeric
12 oz butter
6 oz very cold water

Pastry:
To make the pastry use the directions for Puff Pastry on page 106. Be sure to add the turmeric

The Filling:

In a large pan, heat butter. Add the chopped onion and cook until soft roughly 4 minutes

Add garlic and ginger then cook 1 minute

Add ground beef, turmeric, cumin, cinnamon, cardamom, hot pepper and thyme

Cook until beef is browned roughly 10 minutes

Add green onions, parsley, tomatoes and beef stock then simmer for 25 minutes or until

most of the liquid has evaporated

Add salt and pepper to taste

Remove from heat. Add rum and puree in food processor then let cool before assembling patties

To make the patties:

Preheat oven to 400 degrees

On a lightly floured surface roll out pastry to a thickness of 3/16"

Cut pastry into 6 – 7" circles

Spoon ¼ cup cooled meat filling onto the center of one side of each circle

Brush the edges of the circle with the egg wash mixture

Fold the other half of the pastry over so the edges meet

Use a fork to crimp the edges together

Lightly brush the top of each patty with the egg wash

Place the patties on a wax paper lined baking sheet and bake until golden brown about 30 minutes. Serve hot.

For the snack / appetizer size:

Divide pastry dough into 2 pieces

Roll pastry into 2 sheets 3/16" thick

Place several 1 tbsp portions of meat mixture onto the dough 1 ½" apart

Brush with the egg wash around the meat

Place the second sheet of the pastry on top of the other sheet with the meat

Form and cut into 2" squares crimping the edges with a fork

Brush tops with egg wash and cook as above

More comments from The Garrison Inn

July / 5 / 2007
Our second stay here. Another wonderful visit in your beautiful home with interesting and beautiful decorating, delicious food and spectacular scenery. Hope to be back again. Much happiness in your loving home in the future.   *Jerry & Ethel, Sun City AZ*

July / 17 / 2007
Thanks for making one of the best trips of our lives even better! You're home is beautiful and your hospitality was over the top. You have inspired us to figure out a way to make it back to Montana and make it our home too! I hope our paths will cross again.   *Brenda & Greg, Valtadoros, MI*

July / 26 / 2007
Thank you for the wonderful hospitality! We felt a part of your family. Thanks for the warm welcome; the food and beer/wine were wonderful. The view is magnificent! I really enjoyed watching the sunrise over the mountains. The breakfast was unbelievable! It's like a 5 star restaurant! If ever in SC come visit us.   *June & Eddie, Prosperity, SC*

July / 24 / 2008
We came here by accident but it was the best accident ever! Your home, the view and your hospitality were great and we really enjoyed the evening with the pool table and the delicious house made wine. Also we will never forget Gray's magic tricks and hope we will ever see him in Vegas.
       Leo, Helen, Sander & Rian, The Netherlands

July / 31 / 2008
We were so fortunate to find you through the Internet by searching for "dog friendly places". What a special place, from the beauty of the home and location to the hospitality. I can see you truly love visiting with people. Hope to have you visit Colorado sometime so we can act as hosts.
Tonja, Grand Jct, CO

August / 14 / 2008
Thank you so much for a beautiful, wonderful stay. As I've said, this is by far the greatest B & B we stayed in! The location, your amazing home & hospitality are what make it so fantastic. I feel like friends already! Thanks again for everything and I hope we meet again soon!
James & Kelly, Denver, CO

CRAB CAKES WITH REMOULADE SAUCE

These are a great and impressive appetizer and can be prepped well in advance.

Ingredients:	Remoulade:
2 tbsp olive oil	Juice of 2 lemons
2 celery stalks chopped	½ cup mayonnaise
¼ cup chopped green onion	½ cup chopped green onion
½ cup chopped yellow onion	½ cup chopped yellow onion
1 lb. crab meat	¼ cup chopped celery
1/3 cup dry breadcrumbs	2 garlic cloves chopped
1/3 cup Panko or Japanese breadcrumbs	2 tbsp horseradish
2 tbsp chopped parsley	3 tbsp Dijon mustard
½ cup mayonnaise	1 tsp salt
4 dashes Tabasco	Dash of fresh ground pepper
Salt and pepper to taste	3 tablespoons chopped parsley
3 tbsp butter	

For the crab cakes:

Heat the oil in a sauce pan. Sauté yellow onion and celery until tender roughly 5 minutes. In a large bowl, combine cooked celery, onions and remaining ingredients. Use 1/3 to 1/2 cup of the mixture to form patties Chill at least 1 hour or up to 1 day. Working in batches, heat 1 tbsp butter in a sauce pan and cook crab cakes on each side until golden brown. Place 2 crab cakes on a plate and drizzle with remoulade

For remoulade:
Add all ingredients to a food processor. Mix until well blended. Chill at least 1 hour or up to 1 day
Makes 4 – 6 appetizers

BAKED ALMOND BRIE

Brie is a soft cheese that melts well and makes for a great appetizer. It is best with a Black Currant sauce, but other berries can be substituted.

Ingredients:

1 small Brie wheel

½ cup crushed almond pieces

1 tbsp brandy

1 egg

Flour

½ cup dry bread crumbs

8oz Black Currant jam

1 tbsp butter

1/3 cup water

Melba toast, baguette slices or crackers

Pre heat oven to 350 degrees

Cut Brie into 1" wedges

Combine almond pieces and bread crumbs

Beat egg and add water to make an egg wash

Dredge Brie pieces in flour

Dip Brie pieces in egg wash

Coat Brie with bread crumb and almond mixture

Arrange Brie on a baking sheet. Bake 5 – 10 minutes until cheese starts to melt

Meanwhile, in a sauce pan, melt the jam over medium heat

Thin the jam with the brandy. Add the butter and stir until melted

On small plates make a puddle with sauce covering roughly ½ the plate

Add several pieces of the baked brie to the plate then top with more sauce

Add cracker / toast

Garnish with mint leaves (optional)

Makes 4 appetizers

BRUSCHETTA

Ah, the bounty of summer! Italian Bruschetta is a wonderful way to capture the flavors of summer, with ripe tomatoes, fresh garden basil, and garlic.

Ingredients:

½ loaf French baguette

1 tbsp olive oil

1 tsp Balsamic vinegar

2 tsp chopped garlic

3 ripe Roma tomatoes

1/3 cup chopped onion

8 - 10 fresh basil leaves

3 tbsp olive oil

Heat griddle

Slice the baguette in into ¼" slices

Brush baguette slices on both sides with 3 tbsp olive oil

Grill on both sides until lightly browned

Quarter tomatoes and remove seeds

Chop tomatoes and place in a bowl

Chop basil and add to tomatoes

Add garlic, 1 tbsp olive oil, balsamic vinegar and onion

Toss well

On a plate arrange the grilled bread and top with the tomato mixture

Serves 4 – 6

FRIED CALAMARI

Calamari is a breaded or battered deep fried baby squid, often served with some form of sauce. We like a sweet red chili sauce, but tzatziki is nice too.

Ingredients:

8 oz squid tubes and tentacles
¼ cup chopped red onion
1/3 cup sweet red chili sauce
1 egg
¼ cup water
½ cup flour
½ cup Panko bread crumbs

Preheat deep fryer to 350 degrees
Cut squid tubes into ¼" rings
Toss squid in flour
Make egg wash by combining egg and water
Dip squid in egg wash then bread crumbs
Deep fry squid 45 seconds in hot oil
DO NOT OVER COOK!!!
Plate calamari and top with chopped onions
Serve with the sauce

Serves 4

ONION BHAJJI

Onion bhajji is a spicy East Indian snack consisting of fried onions, for which there are many different recipes. It is often eaten as a starter to main East Indian cuisine courses.

Ingredients:

2 large onions thinly sliced
½ cup vegetable oil
1 cup flour
¼ tsp cumin
2 tsp salt
½ tsp garlic salt
¼ tsp cardamom
¼ tsp turmeric
½ tsp paprika
½ tsp onion powder

Heat oil in wok
Mix flour and all spices together
Toss onions in flour mixture
Once oil is very hot (almost smoking) fry onions in batches
Fry until golden brown and let drain on paper towel
Serve hot

Serves 4 - 6

Sunrise at The Garrison Inn

Main Dishes and Accompaniments

BURRITOS

Mexican food is not just for Cinco de Mayo in our house. We have some form of Mexican cuisine a couple times a month and this is one of the easier dishes to make.

Ingredients:

6 flour tortillas (see recipe page 98)

¼ cup taco seasoning

1 head leaf lettuce

1 can refried beans

1 cup guacamole

1 cup sour cream

1 lb ground beef

¾ cup water

1 medium tomato

1 cup shredded cheddar cheese

1 cup salsa

Make home made tortillas or use store bought

Keep tortillas warm

Brown the beef in a large sauté pan

Drain any fat

Return to heat

Add taco seasoning and water

Simmer until liquid evaporates

Place 2 tbsp refried bean in each tortilla and spread across middle

Add 3 tbsp meat filling on top of the beans

Add 3 tbsp cheese on top of the meat

Roll tortillas closed

On a plate, place some lettuce, then the burrito

Top with guacamole, tomatoes, salsa and sour cream

Makes 6 burritos

CHICKEN ENCHILADAS

An enchilada is a tortilla rolled around a filling and covered with a chili pepper sauce. Enchiladas can be filled with a variety of ingredients including meat, cheese, beans, potatoes, vegetables, seafood or combinations.

Ingredients:

6 tortilla shells (see recipe page 98)

1 lb boneless, skinless chicken breast

¼ cup taco spice

¾ cup water

8 oz tomato sauce

8 oz salsa

1 cup shredded cheddar and pepper jack cheese mixed

Cut chicken into bite size pieces

In a frying pan cook chicken

Remove chicken from pan and shred in food processor

Return chicken to pan

Add taco spice and water

Simmer until liquid evaporates

Remove from heat and let cool

Preheat oven to 375 degrees

In a mixing bowl combine tomato sauce and salsa sauce

Divide meat between the 6 tortillas. Roll tortillas to close

Place in a 9" square cake pan. Top with sauce and cheese

Bake 20 – 30 minutes until cheese melts

Serves 3 – 6

BEEF QUESADILLAS

Quesadillas are a Mexican or Tex/ Mex dish that can be filled with a variety of ingredients with cheese being the primary ingredient.

Ingredients:

4 tortilla shells

1/8 cup taco spice

½ cup water

1 (4 oz) can green chilies

½ cup salsa

1 ½ cups shredded cheddar and mozzarella cheese

8 oz ground beef or left over prime rib, roast beef, etc.

12 jalapeño pepper rings

½ cup sour cream

¼ guacamole

Preheat griddle to 425 degrees

Brown ground beef or run the left over beef through food processor then place in a sauté pan

Add taco spice and water to the meat

Simmer until liquid evaporates, set aside

Chop the jalapenos

On 2 of the tortillas spread the meat

Top with the green chilies and the jalapenos

Top with the cheese and the other tortillas

Grill until lightly browned on each side

Cut each quesadilla into 6 pieces

Plate and serve with sour cream, salsa and guacamole

Serves 4 – 6

CHICKEN CHIMICHANGA

The Chimichanga is a fried burrito that can be filled with a wide range of ingredients: beans, meat, vegetables etc.

Ingredients:

6 flour tortillas (see recipe page 98)
¼ cup taco seasoning
1 head leaf lettuce
1 can refried beans
1 cup guacamole
1 cup sour cream

1 lb diced chicken
¾ cup water
1 medium tomato
1 cup shredded cheddar cheese
1 cup salsa
¼ cup oil

Make home made tortillas or use store bought
Keep tortillas warm
Brown the chicken in a large sauté pan
Add taco seasoning and water
Simmer until liquid evaporates
Heat oil in large frying pan
Place 2 tbsp refried beans in each tortilla and spread across middle
Add 3 tbsp meat filling on top of beans
Add 3 tbsp cheese on top of meat
Fold in sides then roll tortillas closed
Fry in hot oil until browned on all sides
On a plate, place some lettuce, then the chimichangas
Top with guacamole, tomatoes, salsa and sour cream

Makes 6 chimichangas

CHICKEN ALFREDO

Do your exercises before and definitely after this dish! Low in fat it is not, but high in flavor it is.

Ingredients:

2 boneless skinless chicken breasts

1 lb fettuccine

1 cup heavy cream (whipping cream)

1 tsp ground white pepper

Fresh parsley for garnish

2 tbsp butter

½ lb butter

1 cup parmesan cheese

1 tsp ground nutmeg

Melt 2 tbsp butter in a frying pan

Dice chicken into bite size pieces

Cook chicken in the frying pan until lightly browned, then set aside

Fill a large sauce pan ¾ full with water and bring to a boil

Meanwhile, in another large sauce pan melt ½ lb of butter

Stir in the cream

Gradually stir in the cheese

Add the pepper and nutmeg

Simmer until the sauce thickens

Add pasta to the boiling water

Cook until tender

Add chicken to Alfredo sauce

Plate pasta and top with sauce

Garnish with parsley

Serves 4

SPATZLE

Spatzle is a German egg noodle / dumpling that can be served a number of ways: with a little melted butter, fried, or Gray's favorite, with cheese, ham and green onion.

Ingredients:

4 eggs

½ cup water

1 tsp ground white pepper

3 – 3 ½ cups flour

½ cup chopped green onions

1 cup shredded mozzarella and cheddar cheese mixed

1 cup of milk

1 tsp salt

1 tsp nutmeg

3 tbsp oil

½ cup diced ham

Fill a large sauce pan ¾ full of water and bring to a boil

In a large mixing bowl beat the eggs

Add the milk, water, salt, pepper and nutmeg

Gradually mix in flour until you get a thick batter

If you have a spatzle maker pour some of the batter into it then drizzle the batter into the boiling water

If you don't have a spatzle maker you can use a ricer or a whisk to drizzle the batter

Spatzle is done when it floats

If you are going to serve it with butter, take the hot spatzle and toss it with melted butter then serve

If you are going to fry it, the spatzle is easier to work with if you let it cool

For fried spatzle, heat 3 tbsp oil in a frying pan

Add spatzle, season with salt and pepper and fry until lightly browned

For Gray's favorite, toss in the ham, onions and cheese with the fried spatzle and bake for 5 minutes or until the cheese melts

FETTUCCINE CARBONARA

A great, rich and creamy sauce to serve over any pasta, but I like it best over fettuccine.

Ingredients:

1 lb fettuccine

1 large onion

1 cup heavy cream (whipping cream)

1 tsp ground white pepper

Fresh parsley for garnish

½ lb bacon

½ lb butter

1 cup parmesan cheese

1 tsp ground nutmeg

Dice bacon into bite size pieces

Finely chop the onion

Cook the bacon until lightly browned then set aside

Cook the onions in the bacon fat until tender then set aside

Fill a large sauce pan ¾ full with water and bring to a boil

Meantime in another large sauce pan melt the butter

Stir in the cream. Gradually stir in the cheese

Add the pepper and nutmeg

Simmer until the sauce thickens

Add pasta to the boiling water

Cook until tender

Add bacon and onions to the sauce

Plate pasta and top with the sauce

Garnish with parsley

Serves 4

SHRIMP SCAMPI

This is a butter and a garlic lover's delight, and my favorite way to make shrimp. Great over pasta or as a meal.

Ingredients:

1 lb peeled and deveined shrimp
½ cup dry white wine
½ cup butter
3 tbsp olive oil
3 tbsp minced garlic
¼ tsp paprika
1 tbsp chopped parsley
Parmesan cheese

In a large sauté pan melt the butter
Add the oil, garlic, paprika, parsley and wine
Bring to a boil
Add the shrimp and cook until shrimp are pink
Shrimp are done when they form a "C" shape (an "O" shape is over-cooked)
Plate with the sauce and top with a sprinkle of cheese

Serves 2

BEER BATTERED FISH & CHIPS

The batter is simple and easy to make and is a must if you are going to make English style fish and chips.

Ingredients:

1 ½ cups flour
1 egg
1 tsp salt
1 tsp paprika
1 tsp baking soda
12 oz English style dark or amber beer
6 (4 oz) pieces of cod

Preheat deep fryer to 350 degrees
Pour the beer into a mixing bowl
Add egg and beat
Add salt, baking soda and paprika
Gradually stir in flour
Beat until batter is light and frothy
Dust fish with flour
Dip in batter
Fry until golden brown on both sides
Serve with French fries

SEA SCALLOPS WITH AN ORANGE SHERRY SAUCE

Moist and juicy with lots of favor plus quick and easy to make.

Ingredients:

1 ½ lbs large sea scallops

½ cup flour

½ cup olive oil

1 ½ tbsp lemon juice

1 tbsp dry sherry

¼ cup orange juice

4 oz butter

1 tbsp orange zest

3 egg yokes

½ cup melted butter

6 whole dried chili peppers

¼ cup white wine

1 tbsp sherry vinegar or red wine vinegar

1 small shallot minced

Salt and pepper to taste

For the Sauce:

Combine wine, sherry, vinegar, orange juice, shallots and zest in a medium sauce pan and bring to a boil. Reduce heat and cook 3 – 4 minutes until reduced to a syrupy consistency. Reduce heat to very low and whisk in the 4 oz butter 1 tbsp at a time. Season with salt and pepper. Cover and keep warm until ready to serve

For the Scallops:

Preheat oven to 200 degrees. Whisk the egg yokes with 2 tbsp water. In a large sauté pan heat, ¼ cup butter and ¼ cup oil. Cook 3 of the chili peppers until they start to brown then discard the peppers. Rinse and pat dry the scallops. Dip the scallops in the egg yoke then dust with flour. Add half of the scallops to the hot oil and cook each side until golden brown roughly 3 minutes each side. Remove scallops and place in oven to keep warm. Repeat with the remaining chilies adding more oil and butter as needed for the rest of the scallops. Plate the scallops and sprinkle with lemon juice and top with the sauce.

Serves 4

BEEF WELLINGTON WITH BORDELAISE SAUCE

Great family meal for special occasions or one to impress the in-laws or your spouse.

Ingredients:

For Wellington:

1 (3lb) whole beef tenderloin roast
1 tbsp melted butter
1 sheet puff pastry see page (106 for the recipe or use frozen)
½ medium onion finely minced
4 oz finely chopped mushrooms
1 finely chopped shallot
½ tsp dried thyme
½ tsp salt
¼ tsp pepper
2 tbsp brandy
4 oz Braunschweiger liver sausage or liver pate
2 tbsp butter
1 egg separated

For Bordelaise sauce:

3 tbsp butter
1 tbsp minced onion
3 tbsp flour
1 tbsp chopped parsley
¼ tsp thyme
pepper to taste
2 cups beef broth
½ cup red wine

Preheat oven to 425 degrees. Brush roast with melted butter. Roast tenderloin to 120 degrees (very rare), roughly 30 minutes. Let stand 30 minutes. Meanwhile in a frying pan melt 2 tbsp butter. Cook onions until tender. Add shallots and cook 1 minute. Add mushrooms, thyme, salt and pepper. Cook until all liquid evaporates. Add brandy then cook until mixture is dry. Let cool. Spread pate onto cooked tenderloin. Spread mushroom mixture onto puff pastry. Place tenderloin onto mushroom mixture. Fold pastry over tenderloin and seal edges with egg white. Cut trimmings off (These can be used for decorating the Wellington.) Make egg wash with egg yoke and 2 tbsp water. Brush Wellington with egg wash. Bake Wellington 10 minutes then reduce heat to 375 degrees and bake until crust is golden brown. Let stand 15 minutes before slicing.

For the Bordelaise Sauce:

Melt butter in a sauce pan. Cook onions until tender. Add flour and cook until lightly browned.

Add parsley, thyme and pepper. Stir in beef broth and wine. Cook until sauce thickens.

Serve over sliced Wellington.

Serves 4 - 6

COQ AU VIN

This is Anne Marie's contribution to the cook book. Coq Au Vin is a French chicken fricassee with red wine, bacon and mushrooms.

Ingredients:

1 (2 – 3 lb) chicken

2 tbsp olive oil

4 tbsp brandy

1 bay leaf

¼ tsp thyme

12 small button mushrooms

Salt and fresh ground pepper to taste

3 tbsp butter

4 slices of bacon, diced

1 cup red wine

2 minced garlic cloves

12 pearl onions or ½ cup chopped white onion

2 tbsp flour

2 tbsp chopped fresh parsley or 1 tbsp dried

Cut chicken into 2 thighs, 2 skin-on breasts, 2 wings and the back

Save the back for a chicken stock

Heat 2 tbsp butter and oil in large frying pan

Brown chicken on all sides

Add bacon and brown lightly

Add brandy to pan and ignite, moving pan back and forth until flame goes out

Add wine, bay leaf, garlic, thyme, onions and salt and pepper to taste

Cover and simmer 20 minutes

Meanwhile create a roux by browning 1 tbsp flour in 1 tbsp butter until golden

Add mushrooms and parsley to pot and simmer until chicken is tender 5 – 10 minutes

Transfer chicken to serving dish and keep warm

Add roux to pot to thicken sauce. Pour sauce over chicken

Serves 4

PIEROGIES

Most people believe pierogies are of Slavic origin, but they can be found throughout Eastern Europe and can be made with a variety of fillings.

Ingredients:

2¼ cups flour	1 tsp salt
1 tbsp melted butter	1 cup sour cream
1 egg	1 egg yoke
1 tbsp vegetable oil	4 large Russet potatoes
1 cup shredded cheddar cheese	½ tsp onion salt
Salt & pepper to taste	1 lb bacon
1 medium sized yellow onion	

In a large bowl mix the flour and salt. In a separate bowl whisk together butter, oil, sour cream, egg and egg yoke. Stir the wet ingredients into the flour until well blended. Cover the bowl and let stand 15 – 20 minutes. Peel and cube potatoes then place in a medium sauce pan and cover with water. Bring to a boil and cook until tender roughly 15 minutes. Drain and then mash the potatoes with the cheese. Season with onion salt and salt and pepper to taste. Set aside to cool. Roll the dough out onto a lightly floured surface to 1/8". Cut the dough into 3" circles. Spoon 1 tbsp of the potato filling onto each circle. Brush the edges of the circle with water then fold over into half circles. Press to seal the edges. Place on a cookie sheet and freeze.

To cook pierogies:
Bring a large pot of water to a boil. Dice the bacon and onion then fry. Remove the bacon and onion from the grease and set aside. Boil pierogies until they float. Fry the pierogies in the bacon fat until lightly browned. Plate the pierogies and top with the bacon and onions. Serve with sour cream.

BUNLESS BURGER OVER SPINACH SALAD

I started doing this dish when I was dieting, but I enjoyed it so much, it has become a regular.

Ingredients:

2 oz baby spinach leaves

½ small tomato chopped

3 strips bacon

1 slice Jarlsberg cheese

¼ cup chopped red onion plus 3 sliced rings

1 (6 oz) burger patty

1 oz roasted red pepper salad dressing

Preheat BBQ grill

In a sauté pan cook bacon

Set aside to cool

Grill burger on one side, flip and add the cheese

Cook burger to desired temperature

Meanwhile on a plate spread out the spinach

Top with tomato and onion

Place burger on top of salad

Crumble bacon and sprinkle on top of salad / burger

Drizzle salad dressing over top

Top with sliced onion rings

Serves 1

LAMB SOUVLAKI

Souvlaki is a popular Greek fast food consisting of small pieces of meat and sometimes vegetables grilled on a skewer. It may be served on the skewer for eating out of hand, or in a pita sandwich with garnishes and sauces.

Ingredients:

2 lb. lamb

3 tbsp olive oil

½ tsp freshly ground pepper

2 tsp minced garlic

1 ½ cups shredded leaf lettuce

1 medium onion chopped

Tzatziki (see page 102 for the recipe)

¼ cup lemon juice

½ tsp salt

1 tsp dried oregano

¼ cup minced onion

1 tomato chopped

Flat bread (see page 104 for the recipe)

Cut the lamb into 1" cubes

Place meat into a ziplock bag

Meanwhile mix together lemon juice, oil, salt, oregano, garlic and onions

Pour over meat and let marinate 2 hours or overnight

Preheat grill

Skewer the meat and grill until browned on all sides

Heat flat bread or make fresh

Fill flat bread ½ full with shredded lettuce

Top with grilled meat

Top with chopped tomatoes, onions and Tzatziki

Serves 4 – 6

MONTE CRISTO

The Monte Cristo is a variation of the French croque-monsieur sandwich. Traditionally it is dipped in its entirety in batter and fried. The sandwich is often served with fresh fruit or with clotted cream on the side. I serve it with strawberry jam and sour cream.

Ingredients:

4 boneless, skinless chicken breasts

4 oz sliced Swiss cheese

2 eggs beaten

½ cup half & half

¼ cup sour cream

4 oz sliced Black Forest ham

1 loaf French bread frozen

1 tbsp brandy

¼ cup strawberry jam

In a sauté pan cook chicken breasts

Let cool, then slice

Heat griddle

Microwave bread 30 seconds until soft, but still slightly frozen

Cut bread into ½" slices, keeping slices in order

Microwave bread an additional 30 seconds or until thawed

Take 2 side-by-side slices and top with cheese, ham, then chicken on one slice then cover with other slice

Continue forming sandwiches until the bread is gone

In a cake pan or shallow dish add eggs, brandy and half & half then mix together

Dip sandwiches in egg mixture making sure to cover both sides

Cook on hot griddle until browned on one side

Turn and cook the other side

In a small ramekin place a tbsp of sour cream and jam to serve with the sandwich

Makes 4 - 6 sandwiches

PANZAROTTI

Panzarotti are pockets of dough stuffed with ingredients like cheese, tomato sauce, vegetables, and cured meats before being sealed and fried. You could consider the panzarotti a softer, fried version of the calzone.

Ingredients:

1 tsp sugar

1 package of active dry yeast

1 tsp salt

1 ½ cups your favorite tomato / spaghetti sauce

½ cup mushrooms

½ cup sliced onions

1 cup shredded mozzarella cheese

1 cup lukewarm water

¼ cup olive oil

2 ½ cups flour

½ cup sliced pepperoni or your preferred meat

½ cup green peppers

Or any combination of toppings

Add ½ cup warm water to a large mixing bowl. Stir in the sugar until it dissolves

Sprinkle with yeast and let stand 10 minutes. Add remaining water, oil and salt

Gradually mix in flour. Knead until dough is soft and smooth

Place in a greased bowl and let rise 30 minutes or until doubled

Heat deep fryer to 350 degrees

Punch down dough and divide into 6 pieces

Roll out each piece to 6 "circles 1/2'" thick, cover ½ of each circle with tomato sauce

Top the sauce with the meat and vegetables then top the vegetables with the cheese

Fold over and crimp closed

Deep fry until golden brown on each side

Serve with remaining tomato/ spaghetti sauce heated on the side

Serves 4 - 6

FILET MARIMBA

This is one of the most tender, flavorful steaks of all time. Our absolute favorite!!

Ingredients:

4 (6 – 8 oz) tenderloin filets
½ cup cheddar cheese
½ cup jack cheese
2 tbsp butter
3 tbsp minced garlic
1/8 cup diced hot banana pepper rings

Preheat grill
Shred cheeses and mix together
Melt butter in a sauce pan
Add garlic and hot peppers
Sauté 3 – 5 minutes
Set aside
Butterfly steaks by cutting 90% through and folding open
Spread garlic / pepper mixture over 1 side of each steak
Cover garlic / pepper mixture with cheese
Close steak and skewer together
Grill to desired temperature

CRAYFISH GUMBO

This is a hearty Creole stew with lots of flavor and a touch of spice. If you can't find crayfish, you can substitute shrimp.

Ingredients:

½ cup flour

1 medium onion finely chopped

1 ½ cups sliced okra

¼ cup fresh chopped parsley

3 tbsp Creole seasoning

8 garlic cloves minced

2 cups crayfish tails

1 tsp Tabasco

¼ cup vegetable oil

8 cups water

¼ cup green pepper finely chopped

¼ cup chopped celery leaves

2 tsp salt

1 (14.5 oz) can stewed tomatoes

1 cup crabmeat

6 cups hot cooked rice

Heat oil in a large pot

Add onions and sauté until tender 4 – 5 minutes

Stir in flour and cook 12 – 15 minutes until flour has browned

Gradually stir in water

Add okra, green pepper, parsley, celery leaves, Creole seasoning, salt, garlic and stewed tomatoes

Bring to a boil

Reduce heat and simmer 1 hour

Stir in crayfish, crabmeat and Tabasco

Bring to a boil, reduce heat and simmer 25 minutes

Serve gumbo with rice

KASHMIRI CHICKEN CURRY

To eat an East Indian meal is an experience in itself, with subtle spice blends and exquisite flavors.

Ingredients:

8 oz boneless, skinless chicken breast

1 tbsp green curry paste

1 large potato

1 tbsp oil

3 kaffir lime leaves

¼ cup peas

Hot cooked rice and/or flat bread

1 (5 oz) can coconut milk

1 tbsp red curry paste

1 tbsp butter

1 cup chicken stock

1 fresh red chili pepper

¼ cup corn

In a large pan heat butter and oil

Cut the chicken into bite size pieces

Add chicken to pan and cook until tender

Add coconut milk to pan

Dice potato and add to pan

Add chicken stock, curry paste, lime leaves, corn and peas to pan

Stir well and cook until curry thickens and potatoes are tender

Remove lime leaves

Julienne the pepper and add to the pan and stir

Serve with rice and/or flat bread

Serves 2 -4

A nice variation of this curry is to use all green curry paste. It makes it just a little spicier.

CHAMPAGNE CHICKEN WITH MUSTARD SAUCE

This is a great seasonal dish for the summer. In July in Northwest Montana, wild onions pop up and are wonderful in this dish.

Ingredients:

1 (2 – 3 lb) chicken

½ cup champagne

2 tbsp Dijon mustard

1 tsp fresh ground pepper

2 tbsp finely chopped wild onions

(You can substitute shallots)

6 oz butter

1 ½ cups chicken stock

1 tsp salt

1 tbsp chopped fresh parsley

Preheat oven to 400 degrees

Cut chicken into 2 thighs, 2 skin-on breasts, 2 wings and the back

Season both sides of the chicken pieces with salt and pepper

Place chicken back in a sauce pan with chicken stock

Bring to a boil and continue cooking until reduced to 1 cup

Melt butter in large oven-proof frying pan

Add remaining chicken to frying pan and brown on both sides

Transfer pan to oven and bake 30 minutes

Remove pan from oven and add onions, parsley and champagne

Bake an additional 20 minutes

Make sure the stock is boiling. Stir the mustard into the stock

Add the stock to the frying pan and bake an additional 20 minutes, basting periodically

Plate the chicken and pour the sauce over the chicken

Enjoy with a glass of champagne!!!

Serves 4

LAMB FETA

We often buy a boneless leg of lamb, and then cut it into cutlets, which works well for this recipe.

Ingredients:

1 (8 – 10 oz) lamb cutlet

1 cup diced soft bread cubes

¾ cup diced feta

1 tsp dried basil

1 tsp rosemary

½ tsp thyme

¼ tsp ground white pepper

¾ tsp salt

1 cup beef stock

¼ cup diced onion

¼ cup diced tomato

½ tsp dried basil

¼ cup port

1/3 cup water

3 tbsp corn starch

Preheat oven to 375 degrees

With a mortis and pestle or a spice grinder, crush the 1 tsp basil, rosemary and thyme. Mix together bread, salt, pepper, feta and the crushed spices. Place stuffing on lamb cutlet and roll to close. Tie the roast closed with butcher twine. Roast the lamb 20 minutes. Let stand 5 minutes before cutting. Meanwhile in a sauce pan bring the beef stock to a boil. Add the onions, tomatoes, ½ tsp basil and port. Reduce heat and simmer 15 minutes. Strain sauce and return to heat and bring to a boil. Mix the corn starch in cold water. Stir into the sauce to thicken. Cut the roast into ½" slices. Spoon a small amount of the sauce onto the plate. Top with the cut lamb then top with sauce.

Serves 2

HUNTER STYLE VEAL SCHNITZEL

Hunter style schnitzel is a Wiener schnitzel with a hearty, creamy mushroom sauce.

Ingredients:

1 lb veal cutlets

½ cup bread crumbs

2 tbsp butter

½ cup chopped onion

1 ½ cups beef stock

¼ tsp thyme

1 tbsp chopped parsley

3 tbsp whipping cream

2 eggs beaten

2 tbsp oil

2 bacon strips diced

4 oz sliced mushrooms

3 tbsp brandy

Salt and pepper to taste

3 tbsp sour cream

Heat oil and butter in sauté pan. Pound cutlets to flatten to 1/8" thick

Season the cutlets with salt and pepper. Dredge cutlets in the beaten eggs

Coat the cutlets with bread crumbs

Place the cutlets in sauté pan and cook until golden brown on each

side roughly 1 -2 minutes / side

Remove from pan and keep warm

Sauté the bacon and onions in the sauté pan until browned

Add mushrooms and sauté 2 – 3 minutes

Add brandy, and ignite moving the pan back and forth until flame goes out

Add beef stock, thyme, sour cream and whipping cream

Simmer 5 minutes

Pour sauce over Schnitzel

Serves 4

FLOUR TORTILLAS

These tortillas are quick and easy and will beat store bought anytime.

Ingredients:

1 ½ cups flour
½ tsp salt
1 ½ tsp baking powder
½ cup warm water

Mix together the flour, baking powder and salt
Gradually stir in the water
Knead the dough roughly 5 minutes
Heat griddle
Cut the dough into 8 pieces
Roll the dough into 8" circles 1/16" thick
Cook the dough until lightly browned on both sides
Keep tortillas warm in a 200 degree oven wrapped in a moist towel until ready to use

Makes 8 pieces

YORKSHIRE PUDDING

Yorkshire pudding is an English dish made from batter. It is most often served with roast beef.

Ingredients:

¾ cup flour

½ tsp salt

2 beaten eggs

1 cup milk

The drippings and fat from a roasted prime rib or 3 tbsp oil and 3 tbsp butter

Mix the flour and salt together

Stir in the eggs and milk

Beat until batter is smooth

Refrigerate 2 hours or more

Preheat oven to 450 degrees

Using a 6 cup muffin pan place a tsp of drippings or butter & oil mixture into each cup

Heat muffin pan in oven for 5 minutes until oil is smoking hot

Remove batter from fridge and beat

Remove pan from oven and pour batter into each cup until ¾ full

Return pan to oven and cook 10 minutes

Reduce heat to 350 degrees and cook 15 – 20 minutes until puddings are puffed up and golden brown

DO NOT OPEN OVEN DOOR WHILE PUDDING IS BAKING AS IT WILL DROP!!!

Serve hot

Makes 6

TZATZIKI

Tzatziki is a Greek meze or appetizer, also used as a sauce for souvlaki and gyros. Tzatziki is made of strained yogurt.

Ingredients:

1 medium cucumber
¼ tsp salt
1 cup plain yogurt
1 tbsp olive oil
1 tsp lemon juice
1 tsp dried oregano
1 tsp garlic

Cut the cucumber in half then remove seeds and finely chop
Place cucumber in a strainer and sprinkle with salt and let drain 1 hour
Place yogurt in strainer and let drain 1 hour
Mix yogurt and cucumber together
Add lemon juice, oil, salt, garlic and oregano
Cover and chill 1 hour

Makes 1 ½ cups

FLAT BREAD

This quick and easy bread has all kind of uses. When a recipe calls for a pita, make this flat bread instead and impress all your friends.

Ingredients:

1 ½ cups flour
½ tsp salt
1 ½ tsp baking powder
½ cup warm water
3 tbsp vegetable oil

Mix together the flour, baking powder and the salt
Gradually stir in the water
Knead the dough roughly 5 minutes
Heat the oil in a large frying pan
Cut the dough into 6 pieces
Roll the dough into 6" circles 3/16" thick
Fry the dough until lightly browned on both sides
Keep warm until ready to use

Makes 6 pieces

PUFF PASTRY

This is a light, flakey and buttery pastry that can be used for a number of dishes.

Ingredients:

2 ½ cups flour	½ tsp salt
12oz butter	6oz very cold water

To make Pastry:

For best results everything needs to be cold so the butter does not melt. Mix flour and salt then freeze for 30 minutes. Cut butter into pieces and freeze 30 minutes. Remove butter and flour from the freezer. On a large surface place the butter and cover with the flour. Using a pastry scraper or a large chef's knife cut the butter into the flour. Work until you have a crumbly mixture. Add the cold water a little at a time to the dough to loosely bind it. Mix the dough until it just hangs together. At this stage it looks as far from dough as is possible. Shape the messy dough into a rectangle and roll it until it's ½" thick. Do not overwork or over water the dough as it will eventually hold together. Use the pastry scraper to fold the dough into thirds like a letter. Don't worry if it folds in pieces. Turn the dough 90 degrees so the folds run vertically. Square off the edges and roll the dough into rectangles to a thickness of ½". Always roll from open end to open end. Continue rolling, folding and turning until dough looks smooth. By four or five turns the dough should hang together well. Fold the smooth dough up like a book. To do this, fold the 2 shorter sides into the middle then fold the dough like a book. Wrap the dough in plastic wrap and refrigerate for 30 minutes. Roll dough to ½" then fold like a letter. Perform two more rolls, folds and turns. Fold the dough like a book. Chill and rest dough for 30 minutes. The dough is now ready to roll to shape and use.

Shape the shaggy dough into a rectangle ½" thick.

The first few folds are messy, don't worry.

Turn the dough 90 degrees.

Continue rolling and folding until dough is smooth.

Fold the dough like a book, brush off excess flour.

Wrap the dough in plastic wrap and chill.

Sweets & Treats

BUTTER BRICKLE

One of my favorite candies growing up. It was a Christmas tradition that I just recently started doing again.

Ingredients:

1 lb. butter
1 ½ cups chopped almonds
2 cups white sugar
12 oz chocolate bits
3 tbsp butter
1/3 cup half & half

Melt 1 lb. butter in medium sauce pan
Stir in sugar
Cook over medium heat until candy thermometer registers 300 degrees
Pour into a 12" x 15" baking sheet and let cool
Chop nuts
Over low heat melt chocolate
Stir in 3 tbsp butter, nuts and the cream
Pour over brickle
Freeze
Once frozen break into pieces
Store in freezer

Serves 1 unless you want to share

SUGAR MOLASSES COOKIES

Remember the cookies your mother always made for you as a kid? Well these are mine, and they are still my favorite. I've been making them for over 30 years.

Ingredients:

¾ cup shortening

1 egg

2 cups flour

1 ½ tsp cinnamon

1 tsp ground ginger

1 cup sugar

¼ cup molasses

1 tsp baking soda

1 tsp ground cloves

½ cup sugar

Preheat oven to 375 degrees

Melt shortening in a medium sauce pan

Add 1 cup sugar and the molasses

Cook until sugar dissolves

Let cool

Beat egg and add to pan

In a separate bowl mix together the flour, baking soda, cinnamon, ginger, and cloves

Stir into the pan

Chill 30 minutes

Roll into 1" balls

Roll balls into the remaining sugar

Arrange balls onto a baking sheet

Bake 12 minutes or until the balls flatten and are golden brown

Store in air tight container

BAKLAVA

Baklava is a rich, sweet pastry made of layers of phyllo dough filled with chopped nuts and sweetened with syrup.

Ingredients:

4 cups chopped walnuts

1 cup brown sugar

2 tsp ground allspice

1 (1 lb) package of phyllo pastry

1 cup honey

2 tbsp grated lemon rind

Juice of 1 orange

2 cups chopped almonds

4 tsp cinnamon

1 ½ cups melted butter

2 cups white sugar

1 ½ cups water

2 tbsp grated orange rind

Preheat oven to 350 degrees

Combine brown sugar, nuts, 2 tsp cinnamon and 1 tsp allspice in a mixing bowl.

Set up a work station with the bowl of nut filling, the melted butter, a pastry brush, an 11" x 17" baking sheet and the phyllo dough. Brush the baking sheet with melted butter. Place a sheet of phyllo dough onto it. If it is larger than your pan, let the edges hang over the sides. Brush the sheet with melted butter. Repeat this process with 4 sheets. Sprinkle some of the nut filling evenly over the pastry. Cover with 2 buttered sheets of dough. Continue this combination until the filling is used up. Top the baklava with 5 sheets of buttered dough. Trim the edges of any excess dough. Score the Baklava into diamond shapes roughly 3" across. Cut down to, but not through the bottom layer. Bake 60 minutes or until golden brown. Meanwhile combine the white sugar, honey, water, lemon rind, orange rind and orange juice in a sauce pan. Bring to a boil and boil until syrup thickens roughly 15 – 20 minutes. Let cool. Remove the Baklava from the oven and re-cut the Baklava. Pour the syrup over the hot Baklava then let cool.

Serve at room temperature

SOUTHERN PECAN PIE

A truly classic southern pie. This recipe comes out every Christmas. Sometimes I add chocolate pieces for a change, or just make one of each.

Ingredients:

1 1/3 cups flour	½ cup shortening
½ tsp salt	4 – 6 tbsp cold water
¼ cup butter	1 cup sugar
1 cup light corn syrup	4 eggs
¼ tsp salt	1 tsp vanilla
3 tbsp bourbon	1 ½ - 2 cups pecans

For the Pie Crust:

Combine flour and salt. Cut in shortening to form a crumbly mixture

Stir in the water 1 tbsp at a time. Form into a ball then flatten dough into ½" thick disk

Wrap with plastic wrap and chill 30 minutes. Roll dough out ¾" larger than pie plate

(I use an 11" flan pan) fold dough in quarters then place in pie pan

Unfold dough and trim off excess

For Filling:

Combine butter, sugar and corn syrup in a medium sauce pan

Cook over low heat until sugar dissolves

Let cool slightly

Beat eggs and add to pan

Stir in salt, vanilla and bourbon

Fill pie shell with pecans. Pour filling over pecans

Bake at 325 degrees for 50 – 55 minutes

CHRISTMAS CINNAMON ROLLS

Cinnamon rolls and champagne on Christmas morning are a tradition in our house. We always make several batches and give them to our neighbors and friends as presents.

Ingredients:

½ cup lukewarm water

1 envelope fast-rising yeast

¼ cup sugar

3 tbsp shortening

1 beaten egg

2 tsp cinnamon

¾ cup chopped walnuts

1 tsp sugar

½ cup scalded milk

½ tsp salt

3 cups flour

1 cup brown sugar

¾ cup seedless raisins

½ cup melted butter

Dissolve 1 tsp sugar in the warm water in a mixing bowl. Add the yeast. Let stand 10 minutes. Scald the milk. Remove from heat. Stir in ¼ cup sugar, salt and shortening then let cool. Stir yeast into the water. Add milk to the yeast mixture. Add eggs. Stir in flour. Knead dough until smooth and elastic. Place in a greased bowl and brush with melted butter. Let rise until doubled. Combine brown sugar, cinnamon, raisins and walnuts. Punch dough down. Roll dough out to a 16" x 12" rectangle ¼" thick. Grease 7 – 8" round cake pans with melted butter. Sprinkle pan with brown sugar mixture. Brush dough with melted butter. Top dough with remaining brown sugar mixture. Roll dough up jelly roll fashion. Cut dough into 1" pieces and place in the cake pans. Brush tops with butter. Let rise until doubled. Preheat oven to 350 degrees. Bake cinnamon rolls 20 – 25 minutes or until golden brown.